THE ILLUSTRATED MOTORCYCLE LEGENDS

Suzuki

ROY BACON

CHARTWELL
BOOKS, INC.

This edition published in 1996 by
CHARTWELL BOOKS, INC
A division of BOOK SALES, INC
P.O. Box 7100
114 Northfield Avenue
Edison, New Jersey 08818-7100

© Text Roy Bacon 1996
© Layout and Design the Promotional Reprint Company Ltd 1996

ISBN 0 7858 0637 7

ACKNOWLEDGEMENTS

The author and publishers wish to acknowledge their debt to Suzuki, whose material has
provided the bulk of the pictures used in this title. Most have been collected by the author
over the years; others were sent on request to complete the story. Also thanks to
Ralph Petts for the picture of his lovely GT750.

FRONT COVER, BACK COVER AND TITLE PAGE:
The GSX-750 in its all-new 1996 form, even faster than before and making the best of
advanced technology

Printed and bound in China

Contents

FOUNDATIONS 1952-1962

Suzuki came to motorcycles in 1952 from a background of loom making and other products. By then the founder, Michio Suzuki, was 63, but wished to see his firm in a stable industry with real prospects of expansion before he retired. Transport, especially low-cost transport, was an excellent choice for the demand in postwar Japan was enormous and foreign competition non-existent.

Michio began, as others had, producing a small engine to fit to a bicycle. The first was the 36cc two-stroke Power Free which was soon enlarged to 50cc and given a two-speed gear. A year later this improved to become the 58cc Diamond Free while the 50cc engine was used by the Mini-Free belt-drive moped of 1954.

Unhappy with the two-stroke engine of the time, the firm turned to four-strokes and side valves for 1954 when the 90cc CO and then the 123cc COX were built. Both were true motorcycles having three speeds, telescopic front forks and plunger rear suspension, but were replaced by the 102cc Porter Free and 123cc ST two-stroke models during 1955 for Suzuki had reappraised its two-stroke knowledge to concentrate on that engine form for the next two decades.

Start of the Suzuki line was a clip-on engine which quickly grew into this 58cc Diamond Free two-speed unit.

Complete Diamond Free of 1953, the machine boasts telescopic front forks but otherwise clearly has bicycle origins.

This 1954 Mini-Free was an early moped with a two-stroke engine and belt drive. SJK stood for Suzuki Jidosha Kogyo.

The four-stroke 123cc COX model, was a real motorcycle but the firm then reverted to two-strokes for the next two decades.

A return to two-stroke engines brought the ST model in 1955, its style much of that era.△

First Suzuki twin was this 1956 247cc Colleda TT model, a marque name used by the firm during that decade.

With its energies directed at one engine type, Suzuki's next move was its first twin, the 247cc Colleda TT of 1956. This differed in other ways for it had four speeds, a pressed-steel frame and leading-link front forks. A year later Michio retired, well pleased with his transport models that now included a 360cc car.

The next model was the Suzumoped, very similar to the highly successful German NSU, and it was soon followed by a 125cc twin and other small motorcycles in an array of forms. This gave the firm a good range of machines from 50 to 250cc which it produced in large numbers. As with the other Japanese firms, Suzuki began to export, gradually increasing the volume.

The Suzumoped had the lines of the German NSU Quickly model but not its two speeds.

Listed as the 125cc Colleda Seltwin of 1959, the model had S for Suzuki on tank and engine covers and was a good performer.

In its early days Suzuki went racing at Mount Fuji and Asama, with limited results, and then attempted the tough Isle of Man TT in 1960. It returned to Europe for 1961, but was off the pace and unreliable so sought out Ernst Degner, a top rider and engineer then working for the East German MZ team. In secret, Degner defected to the West and went to Japan to join Suzuki where he soon had the power and reliability they sought for their engines.

From this started a long and successful grand prix career and the beginnings of the Japanese development of the two-stroke engine. Degner won Suzuki's first world title in 1962: eight more fell to the firm that decade. The technology advanced at amazing speed from the most basic two-stroke to the 1967 twin-cylinder 50cc, disc-valve engine with its 14-speed gearbox. There was also a 50cc triple and 125cc V-Four before the Japanese firms withdrew their factory support for a few years.

As the racing machines became highly sophisticated through the 1960s, so the model range expanded although it kept mainly to small capacities for much of that decade. Many were of 50 or 80cc and were offered in touring, sports, step-thru and trail forms, often in more than one guise. Some of the off-road models had a dual-range gearbox and these gradually enlarged and were joined by enduro and motocross models.

The Colleda as used at Asama in 1959 when the sole Suzuki finisher was fifth on this basic two-stroke.

By 1963 the 125 was a twin with disc inlet valves and rear exhausts but water-cooling was not to come until 1965.

The complex engine unit of the 1967 125, a V-Four driving a 12-speed gearbox and running to 16,500rpm.

This 1962 Selped moped was typical of the Suzuki range at that time, its lines common to many other models.

SETTLING DOWN, SINGLES AND TWINS 1963-1971

Some of the models which appeared in those early days were to have a long life with minimal changes. One such was the step-thru scooterette which began as the 1963 M30, later became the F50 and then the FR50 to be joined by larger versions which ran to the late-1980s. The A100 was similar, being a basic single built from 1967 to 1980, and also in other formats.

Alongside the myriad of small singles ran the twins. From the early Colleda came the T10 in 1963 and the 1966 T20 which was soon known as the Super Six thanks to its six-speed gearbox, high performance and modern construction. In Japan it was also listed as a trail model with raised exhausts.

The following year, 1967, was to herald the start of the move of the Japanese firms to larger machines. In the wings waited Honda's CB750 and Kawasaki's H1 but first came the Suzuki 500/Five, sold as the Titan in the USA and Cobra in Europe but listed as the T500. It was to be overshadowed by the others for its lines were those of the existing twins but it proved a hit with the more discerning customers who found it very fast and completely reliable even if rather thirsty and prone to vibration.

The start of the scooterette line came in 1963 with the M30 that was developed to run for many years.

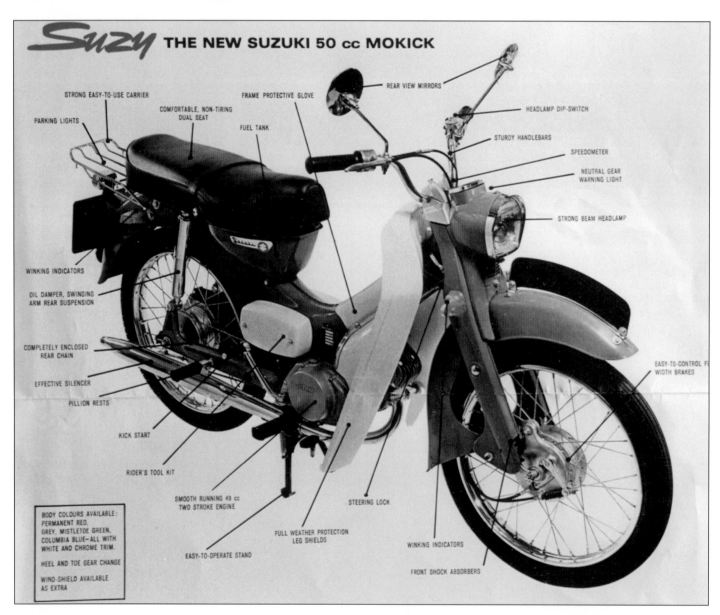

Suzy THE NEW SUZUKI 50 cc MOKICK

STRONG EASY-TO-USE CARRIER

PARKING LIGHTS

COMFORTABLE, NON-TIRING DUAL SEAT

FRAME PROTECTIVE GLOVE

FUEL TANK

REAR VIEW MIRRORS

HEADLAMP DIP-SWITCH

STURDY HANDLEBARS

SPEEDOMETER

NEUTRAL GEAR WARNING LIGHT

STRONG BEAM HEADLAMP

WINKING INDICATORS

OIL DAMPER, SWINGING ARM REAR SUSPENSION

COMPLETELY ENCLOSED REAR CHAIN

EFFECTIVE SILENCER

PILLION RESTS

KICK START

RIDER'S TOOL KIT

EASY-TO-CONTROL F WIDTH BRAKES

SMOOTH RUNNING 49 cc TWO STROKE ENGINE

STEERING LOCK

BODY COLOURS AVAILABLE:
PERMANENT RED,
GREY, MISTLETOE GREEN,
COLUMBIA BLUE—ALL WITH
WHITE AND CHROME TRIM.

HEEL AND TOE GEAR CHANGE

WIND-SHIELD AVAILABLE AS EXTRA

EASY-TO-OPERATE STAND

FULL WEATHER PROTECTION LEG SHIELDS

WINKING INDICATORS

FRONT SHOCK ABSORBERS

The A100 was a long-running basic model with simple two-stroke, disc-valve engine, pump lubrication and four speeds.

Another single listed for a decade was this B120. First seen in 1967 as shown it was a simple, basic motorcycle.

Smallest motorcycle in the 1960s was the A50 which had five speeds and a good town performance.

Based on the A100, the A80 differed little other than in managing with just 72cc of capacity.

The scooterette moved on to become the FR50 in time, along with versions with larger engines.

In 1963 the T10 twin replaced the Colleda TT, retaining the capacity and four speeds, but adopting a better frame.

By 1966 the twin had become the T20 Super Six, much more modern in its design and both fast and reliable.

This TC250 was a street scrambler model built for Japan in 1967. It used the T21 engine, a tuned version of the T20.

Opposite above: A T500 twin; fast, very reliable, but with no real style of its own so underrated by everyone except its owners.

Opposite below: In contrast, the T90 twin – which copied a 125cc model known as the Stinger with its layout of engine and exhausts – had style.

By 1969 the twin-cylinder range ran from 90 to 500cc and included engines of 125, 200, 250 and 300cc but, while all performed extremely well, they lacked the attractive image of the opposition's models. Those who bought and rode the twins were more than happy with their choice, but the firm needed something more to lift it to the buyer's attention.

Off-road, Suzuki's machines began to move from being modified road models to more purpose-built forms. Of these, the TC trail series built from 90 to 185cc used the dual-range gearbox but the similar TS models kept to a conventional five speeds. While the TC was dropped in the 1970s, the TS remains in the modern Suzuki list, albeit much altered over the years.

Suzuki went into motocross in the 1960s and by 1970 achieved world dominance in the 250cc class, the 500cc crown falling to them the next year and for several more. In 1975 the firm added the then new 125cc class and won many world titles in all three classes. Encouraged by the early

successes, Suzuki introduced a production version, the TM400 in 1971, but it and the later TM250 and TM125 were not to sell well. Buyers quickly realised that they were more of a trail or enduro machine than a serious competition racer, but this was soon to change.

The TS125 of 1971 had a low exhaust and close fitting front mudguard but ran well on roads or dry trails.

The larger 1971 TS185 Sierra was rather more suited to rough off-road trail riding.

The 1969 TS250 had a raised exhaust but the close mudguard would soon clog if the trail was muddy.

The TS250 is all heart

From 1971 Suzuki listed the TM400 as a motocross model but it was not to be for serious competition. In 1976 it was replaced by the highly successful RM series.

TRIPLES AND THE RE5 1972-1975

The answer to Suzuki's marketing problem came in two forms: the first a trio of three-cylinder models introduced in 1972, the second the RE5 with its rotary engine which arrived two years later. Both moved the firm up and onto a par with their opposition. The triples all followed the same pattern with the three cylinders in line across the frame, a horizontally-split crankcase and the gearbox in unit with the engine.

The GT750 was a step forward for Suzuki, heralding a trio of two-stroke triples, all finely equipped but this one alone was water cooled.

A beautifully restored GT750 of 1976, some two decades on and still called the 'kettle' by its owner, as is usual.

Smallest triple was the GT380 which featured the Ram Air cooling system and was fitted with a six-speed gearbox.

The middle triple was the GT550, fitted with four silencers just as the others, and with five speeds.

New for 1973, the GT185 had its cylinders vertical, kept the Ram Air feature and had electric or kick starting.

The T250 became the GT250 for 1973 and continued the line of such models which go back to the Colleda of 1956.

Smallest twin was this GT125 which replaced the T125 in 1973 and was similar to the GT185 in specification.

Typical of the long running TS series in the early 1970s, this TS100 had a disc-valve, two-stroke engine and five speeds. The TC version had a dual-range, four-speed gearbox.

Trials RL250 model developed by Graham Beamish for Suzuki and also built in RL325 form and with a sidecar.

The first to appear was the largest, the 739cc GT750, and was essentially one-and-a-half T500 engines to which water-cooling had been added. It was launched at the Tokyo show in 1971 and listed as the Le Mans in the USA but was soon nicknamed the 'kettle' by owners, a name that stuck over the years.

Conventional construction was used for the GT750 which was built more as a grand tourer than a superbike and, although quite large, it did its job well. It also proved well able to shed the bulk of its outer coatings to become a lean road racer, and Barry Sheene, among many, had numerous race wins on the model.

By early 1972 the smallest triple, the 371cc GT380 listed in the USA as the Sebring, was on sale, and differed in having six speeds and air cooling, the latter augmented by a cast shield over the cylinder head. Suzuki called this arrangement the 'Ram Air System', and styled it to suit. The machine proved to be fast, thirsty and exciting to ride - so fulfilled its aim. It was soon joined by the 544cc GT550, the Indy in the USA, which was the same only more so as regards performance although different in many engine details and with only five speeds.

From 1973 the twins became GT models in turn, first the 185 and 250, then the 125 and finally the 500. The two smaller adopted the Ram Air cooling, but only the smallest survived into the 1980s as the others were replaced by new designs.

The off-road range continued with its TC, TS and TM models during this period, but they were joined by two other model types. One was a pure trials machine, introduced as the RL250 in 1973, based on the TS series and intended to sell in the USA. When the expected US boom in trials failed to materialise, many were shipped to Britain where Graham Beamish modified them to suit UK trials and was so successful in this that he was given the right to build Suzuki trials models.

The second off-road series was an all-terrain fun model having small diameter wheels shod with fat tyres and able to run on road, mud, sand, dirt or snow. Thus, the RV series was the predecessor to the three or four-wheeled machines that came later, and was offered in 50, 75, 90 and 125cc capacities.

Highlight of the 1974 range, the RE5 was far more radical, and aimed to promote the firm by its use of the new technology of the rotary engine to power a smooth, sophisticated grand tourer with a hint of sports performance. Notionally of 500cc, it used the Wankel engine concept that originated from NSU in Germany, and was used by a few firms for both cars and motorcycles, but with limited success.

The RE5 turned out to be a large motorcycle using a conventional chassis but a new engine shape. The basic principle was simple but the technology complex and the engine ancillaries many while the performance was barely adequate and the fuel consumption very heavy. The model was listed up to 1977 as were the two larger triples, the smaller continuing for two more years.

Suzuki was about to change tack. As Barry Sheene took his works Suzuki RG500 to world titles in 1976 and 1977, the firm began a major switch to the four-stroke engine, although it kept the two-strokes for its very successful motocross machines. In addition, it began to build replicas of Sheene's machine for general sale and these helped to swell the 500cc grids for a number of years, all built in the same format with four cylinders in a square, water-cooled and with disc valves.

The RG500 swelled the racing grids for many years but this one, number 8, is the great Mike Hailwood about to practices on his works machine on which he won the Senior.

FOUR STROKES 1976-1980

Suzuki stunned its customers when it announced the 1976 range for it included the GS750, a model with a four-cylinder, twin overhead camshaft, four-stroke engine in what had become the stock Japanese format from rivals Honda and Kawasaki. The machine was conventional for its day, the engine built in unit with the five-speed gearbox and fed by four carburettors, the frame tubular with telescopic front and pivoted-fork rear suspension, disc brakes front and rear, and fully equipped including electric start.

First Suzuki four-stroke four was the GS750 which proved to be right up with the other Japanese makes from its launch.

Half the four, stretched a little, produced the GS400 twin as a fine mid-range model with an excellent specification.

The new four-strokes were quickly joined by the GS550 four which went on to be highly popular with riders.

Suzuki introduced its successful RM series of motocross models in 1976, these replacing the TM models; this is the RM250.

The four grew into the GSX1100 for 1978, retaining all the existing features in a 130 plus mph package. This example is from 1981.

A four-stroke, single-cylinder trail model was added to the 1978 range as the SP370, well able to perform on road or rough track.

Suzuki's first 4-stroke, single cylinder dual purpose bike

For 1978 the 250cc twin-cylinder, two-stroke was much altered to become the X7 with reed-valves, six speeds and less weight.

In 1979 the X7 was joined by the smaller 200cc X5 which duplicated it in many ways.

Along with the X5 came the SB200, a sober model with wire wheels and drum front brake in place of the alloys and disc.

With the four came a twin, the GS400 which was of similar appearance and specification other than for a six-speed gearbox and drum rear brake. Otherwise, the style duplicated the four and both models soon proved that Suzuki had done a fine job for they proved to be fast, economical and reliable. Before the year was out they were joined by another four, the GS550, which was to be just as successful.

While the new four-strokes were showing that the firm had no problem with that engine type, the new motocross models of 1976, the RM series, showed that Suzuki had overcome its initial difficulties in that field. The range quickly stretched out from 50 to 400cc and became very successful, to run on right up to modern times with continuing development.

New for 1978 were the GP100 and GP125, very similar and both basic two-stroke singles, this the larger.

Copying the style of the twins, this ZR50 of 1979 was also typed as the X1.

The trail series of two-stroke models extended down to add the TS50 in 1979.

For 1979 the four-stroke twin grew to become the GS425 but was otherwise little altered.

Both more capacity and shaft drive were offered by the GS850 of 1979 which was as the 750 in other respects.

New in 1979 were models having four-valve cylinder heads, the smaller being the four-cylinder GSX750 in a revised style.

The four-stroke range grew further for 1978 when the GS1000 was added in the same format as the others and proved to be a fine machine. The SP370 took the firm in another direction for it was a trail model, but one that fitted a single-cylinder, overhead camshaft engine rather than a two-stroke unit for an alternative approach to off-road riding.

The 250cc two-stroke twin had its style and performance sharpened up for 1978 and became the X7, joined the next year by the similar 196cc X5 whose engine went into the more sober SB200. Also new in 1978 were singles in the form of the very similar GP100 and GP125 while the ZR50 single of 1979 took the new twin style and was badged as the X1, being joined by the TS50 trail model, in the style of its larger brothers.

The larger 16-valve four of 1979 was the GSX1100 which offered a further increase in capacity as well as the 'twin swirl' combustion chambers.

For 1980 there were eight-valve twins, the smaller being the GSX250 which had its own style.

The larger eight-valve twin of 1980 was the GSX400 which adopted the same sporting style.

The big four was listed with shaft drive as the GS1000G for 1980, the original chain drive version continuing to be offered.

When fitted with a cockpit fairing the big four was listed as the GS1000S and kept the chain final drive.

A further stretch took the original four-stroke twin out to become the GS450 in the company style.

The four-stroke trail single grew to the SP400 in 1980 but was little altered in other areas.

There were more four-strokes for 1979, the GS425 a stretch of the 400, and the GS850 which had shaft drive as well as more capacity. Of more technical interest were the GSX750 and GSX1100 for both had 16-valve engines, some revision to the style, and the larger a further increase in capacity. The resulting cylinder head of the four-valve design was said to have a twin swirl combustion chamber (TSCC) and this soon featured in Suzuki advertising. The next year saw the fours joined by similar twins, the GSX250 and GSX400.

Along with the SP400 came the similar DR400 with more suspension travel for enduro work.

The GN400 was also SP400-derived but in a custom mould for boulevard cruising.

There were indeed many new models for 1980 as well as the four-valve twins. Shaft drive went onto the big four to produce the GS1000G while that model became the GS1000S when fitted with a cockpit fairing. The larger twin stretched a little more to become the GS450 while the four-stroke single grew to be the SP400 and was joined by the similar DR400 and the custom GN400

Custom style was offered with four cylinders in the form of the 1980 GS550L with its high bars, stepped seat and fat rear tyre.

The custom twin was this GS250TT which followed the same format and fitted the eight-valve engine.

Custom version of the X1 was this OR50 with its high bars and turned-up seat.

One new scooter for 1980 was the FS50 with a two-stroke engine and automatic, two-speed transmission.

The second new scooter for 1980 was the FZ50 with the same mechanics but different wheels and its own style.

The GP100U was a low cost, economy version of the popular two-stroke single.

models. Continuing the custom style were the GS550L and GS250TT, both based on existing models, and the off-beat OR50. Further scooter styles appeared as the FS50 and FZ50 while the GP100U was a utility version of the existing machine.

Off-road, an enduro series was introduced in 1979 with the PE175 and PE250, essentially motocross machines with lights, and these ran on for many years and stretched to add the PE400 in time. There were also desert racing DS variants for the USA, based more on the trail models,

An enduro series appeared in 1979 based on the motocross models, the smaller model this 1983 PE175; the larger PE250 was similar.

Most Japanese firms listed a Farm Bike which was based on a trail model with carriage racks added.

BEAMISH

RM400T

Largest motocross model of 1980 was this RM400, still air-cooled with conventional, but laid-down, rear-suspension units.

The trail models continued to reflect the motocross trends although they always lagged a little as this 1983 TS185 shows.

The Full-Floater rear suspension system was first used by the works road racing and motocross teams. It then went onto the RM series, this an RM500.

Water cooling is essential to enable a high power two-stroke engine to hold its performance and was seen first on the hard working RM125.

a farm bike was included in the range, and the RL325 joined the smaller trials machine. The TS series ran on and all these machines continued to reflect the firm's success in world class motocross competition. Over the next few years water cooling for the engine and a sophisticated rear suspension system dubbed 'Full-Floater' would appear, at first on the works machines, then the production motocross ones, and then the others, including some road models.

KATANA AND TURBO 1981-1985

There was a new name for 1981, Katana, which introduced an exciting style where fuel tank, seat, side covers and tail were all blended together, in some cases with a cockpit fairing. Initially there were three of them, the GSX1100S which had the more advanced styling, the GS550M, and the GS650G which had shaft drive and was accompanied by the conventional GS650GT. Later came the GSX1000S Katana and the GSX400F, a model with a four-cylinder, 16-valve engine.

Also new for 1981 was the FR50 scooterette, designed to continue that long running series, and the custom GSX400T twin, and ZR50L, another custom version of the X1 but more in the usual style of the type. An alternative to the eight-valve engine remained as the GS450 that was also built as the GS450T with high bars, the GS450L with higher bars and stepped seat and the GS450TX with wire wheels in place of the cast alloy ones.

This extensive range set the firm up for some time but each year brought new models. Among those for 1982 were three with anti-dive front forks, this achieved by linking the hydraulics of the

Largest and most exciting of the Katana series of models for 1981 was the GSX1100S which featured the most radical styling and colour.

The GS550M was less radical but certainly stood out from its contemporaries.

Mid-range Katana model, the GS650, much as the 550.

The conventional GS650GT retained the engine and shaft drive of the Katana model but was not nearly so obvious on the street.

During 1981 the GSX1000S Katana joined the series and had the same radical styling as the 1100.

New for 1981 was the four-cylinder GSX400F which had four-valve heads and offered an alternative to the single or twin-cylinder models.

The scooterette models ran on and on in several capacities, this being the 1983 FR50.

Another custom twin was added for 1981, the GSX400T which copied the lines and style of the 250.

Unlike the OR50, the ZR50L was in a conventional custom style but still based on the X1 model.

brakes and suspension. All were much of the Katana style as for the mid-range models, and the machines were the GSX1100EZ, GSX400EZ and GSX250EZ, the largest a four, the others twins.

In addition, there was the CS50 Roadie scooter with two-stroke engine and three models using a 124cc single-cylinder, overhead camshaft engine. These were road models in plain GS125 form, with wire wheels and drum brakes, or fancy GS125ES form where alloy wheels, disc front brake, electric start and a headlight fairing were all features. In off-road form it became the DR125 and, along with the TS and PE models, was fitted with the Full-Floater rear suspension system. At the other end of the scale, the largest shaft-drive four grew to become the GS1100G.

The custom models could be offered in more than one form as the GS450L shows, similar but with variations from the T type.

A further variation of the mid-range twin was the GS450TX which had wire wheels and the touring dual seat.

Largest of the 1982 models with anti-dive forks was the GSX1100EZ which adopted the Katana style.

Larger twin with anti-dive forks was the GSX400EZ offered in the Katana silver or this red.

Smaller GSX250EZ twin with anti-dive in the Katana silver style and finish.

New 1982 scooter was the CS50 Roadie which had a three-speed automatic transmission among its features.

New four-stroke road single for 1982 was this basic GS125 with wire wheels and drum brakes.

Also new was the de luxe GS125ES version which had cast-alloy wheels, a disc front brake and electric starter.

The line of Roadie scooters grew for 1983 with the addition of the CS80 and CS125 while there was also the CL50, designed especially for the ladies to use. The mid-range saw the arrival of the 16-valve GSX550 in E, ES and EF forms which signified a cockpit, half or full fairing. There was also a 16-inch front wheel, anti-dive front forks and the Full-Floater rear suspension for the box-section frame.

There were two other new models that year, both significant in their way. First was the XN85 Turbo which was Suzuki's approach to a trend that all the Japanese firms investigated. In this case the 673cc four-cylinder engine was used as a basis, a turbocharger added and the result was fitted in the most advanced chassis. As with the others, Suzuki found it to be a complex answer to a simple problem best solved by capacity so it was short lived.

The other model took the company back to its early days for the RG250 Gamma had a twin-cylinder, two-stroke engine. It also had water-cooling, six speeds, an aluminium frame, Full-Floater suspension and a fairing so was a quick motorcycle which also handled very well. More four-stroke fours appeared for 1984, the GSX750 being offered in half ES or full EF fairing form as was the GSX1100.

Off-road, the four-stroke single became the DR125 and had the Full-Floater rear suspension system.

The TS125 for 1982, by when it had the Full-Floater rear suspension system but remained air cooled.

In 1982 the largest shaft drive four was stretched out to become the GS1100G.

The CS80 Roadie scooter joined the CS50 for 1983, it having a similar specification.

The CS125 Roadie scooter was also new for 1983 but fitted the four-stroke single engine from the GS125 while retaining the automatic transmission.

Aimed specifically at the female market, the CL50 was smaller than usual and fully automatic.

For the mid-range market of 1983 Suzuki produced the GSX550 with three alternative fairing styles, this the ES half type.

Most technically advanced 1984 model was the XN85 Turbo which was complex under its Katana styling, but not a real answer.

The RG250 brought a return to a twin-cylinder two-stroke engine, but water-cooled and in a brilliant frame.

For 1984 the GSX750 joined the 550 in being offered with a half fairing or, as here, with a full one in EF form.

The GSX1100E was also offered with a choice of fairings and performed well in all forms thanks to its 16-valve engine.

Code RG500 originally referred to the racing machines but in 1985 this Gamma model was built for the road but retained the square-four, two-stroke engine format.

First seen in 1985, the GSX-R750 was a street-legal, road racing machine and most effective on both road and race track.

Many firms listed a full dress tourer in their range by the 1980s and this was the Suzuki version, the GV1400 carrying all the equipment.

A good number of new models appeared for 1985 while others were modified. One machine was modelled on the racing RG500 and as the RG500 Gamma copied the racer with its four water-cooled cylinders arranged in a square, disc valves, and all the latest trick two-stroke technology. The chassis matched the engine with an aluminium box frame and Full-Floater rear suspension among its many features. There was also a smaller version, the RG400, but this was destined for the highly competitive 400cc class in Japan so only sold in its home market.

The four-stroke equivalent of the RG500 was the GSX-R750, effectively a road racing model carefully modified for road use. Its engine remained air-cooled, but this was supplemented by the lubricating oil, a concept the firm would use again in the future.

The line of four-strokes was joined by the short-lived GSX750Se which was built in the Katana style, although this was on its way out. For the USA there came the GV1400, a full-dress tourer powered by a massive water-cooled, twin-cam, four-cylinder engine and fitted out with all the equipment the name implied. It was listed as the Cavalcade.

For the off-road rider Suzuki introduced water-cooling for the TS series and the DR600 Raider trail model with Paris-Dakar styling. It had a single cylinder and single camshaft but four valves

By 1984 the TS125 had both water-cooling and the Full-Floater rear suspension from the motocross series, as well as the RM styling.

Off-road, the big single was stretched to become the DR600 Raider with a Paris-Dakar style including a large petrol tank.

Race style for the learner market came with the RG125 Gamma model, styled as the 250.

The CP50 and CP80 were a new pair of scooters for 1985, both as fully automatic as they could be.

and five speeds all carried on a Full-Floater rear suspension system. The learner market was offered racing style with the RG125 Gamma which duplicated much from the 250, including its finish and lines, while the CP50 and CP80 were a new pair of scooters.

There was even more performance for 1986 from the GSX-R1100, modelled on the 750, while the GSX-R400 became available but only in very limited numbers, having made its debut in Japan the previous year. It was a super-sports machine built for racing but street legal. For solid work on the road the GS450E appeared, an eight-valve, twin-cam twin of traditional lines but more than adequate performance.

More performance was extracted for the GSX-R1100 of 1986 which combined the power of the large engine with the size of a 750.

The solid, mid-range twin model developed into this GS450E for 1986, combining smooth performance with economy.

CUSTOM AND SLINGSHOT 1986-1989

The final 1986 model was the VS750GL Intruder model, a custom machine using a 45-degree V-twin engine, the same as a Harley-Davidson, but with four-valve heads and water-cooling. There was also shaft drive and the traditional custom style expected for such a model.

More custom models appeared for 1987, the largest the VS1400GL Intruder which kept the 45-degree, V-twin engine, but gave it three-valve heads and air cooling. Four speeds in the gearbox were deemed adequate for this monster which kept the shaft drive and styling of the smaller model. The LS650 Savage kept the same format but its engine had but one cylinder, mounted vertically, with overhead camshaft and four valves. It kept to four speeds but had belt final drive. To make up the series there was the GN250 in the same format other than for five gears and chain drive.

The other new models were performance fours of which two were aimed at the Japanese home market and its competitive 400cc class. One was the GSX-R400R, a super-sports model much as the general type but fitted with a racing seat. The second was the GSX-R400RRSP which was a pure street-legal racing model.

A new custom cruiser form was adopted by Suzuki in 1986 using the traditional V-twin engine, but water-cooled with eight valves, to produce the VS750GL Intruder.

VS1400GL

In 1987 a second V-twin was added as the massive air-cooled VS1400GS Intruder which sat on a very fat rear tyre.

The LS650 Savage was a custom single with its own style, belt final drive and a 'deep sound' exhaust system.

Finally, the largest four was further improved to become the GSX1100F. This was more than a minor revision for the engine was an enlarged version of that used by the GSX-R1100. Thus, it had all the expected features while it shared many parts other than those affected by the increase in bore and stroke. The result was very ample power plus more torque right through the range. The chassis was equally advanced to provide both handling and comfort allied to a fairing whose windscreen could be raised or lowered electrically.

For 1988 the GSX-R750 was revised and added the name 'Slingshot' to its code thanks to a new form of carburettor fitted to it. The engine had its stroke reduced while the whole machine was closely related to the racing models but remained street legal. A GSX600F model appeared, based on the 750 as regards its specification, so it had 16 valves, twin cams, air-plus-oil cooling and a considerable performance. The chassis followed Suzuki practice for their sports machines and included a fairing.

There was also a new trail model for 1988, the DR750 Desert Express also known as DR Big. It was a desert style model powered by a massive 727cc single cylinder engine having four valves

A smaller single in the custom series was this GN250 which was equally at home in town traffic or country cruising.

The largest four became the GSX1100F for 1987, combining power, handling and comfort for travel at any speed.

Opposite above: Revised for 1988, the GSX-R750 was heavily modified in both engine and chassis to become known as the 'Slingshot' model from its carburettors.

Opposite below: A high-technology, mid-range model for 1988 was this GSX600F which copied the 750 in many areas to its benefit.

and an overhead camshaft. Fixtures and fittings were on the lines of the Raider but with more protection for both rider and machine plus a 29-litre fuel tank.

A revised version of the GSX-R1100 joined the range for 1989 and again reflected the latest trends from the racing circuits. Its engine was enlarged to 1127cc and fitted with Slingshot carburettors and a stainless-steel exhaust system, but continued with air cooling supplemented by the lubricating oil that had its own radiator. Five speeds were more than adequate thanks to the massive engine torque while the diaphragm clutch was hydraulically operated. The whole package went into a new aluminium-alloy frame having Full-Floater rear suspension and was enclosed by a full fairing.

The DR750 Desert Express took the concept of the big single further, used motocross-style suspension and had a 29-litre long-range tank.

Slingshot carburettors went onto the GSX-R1100 in 1989 when its capacity was increased among its many improvements.

For 1989 the RGV250 replaced the older twin two-stroke, its engine completely revamped into a compact V-twin in a pure road racing style.

The new 1989 sports model GSX750F which combined the lines of the similar 600 with the larger engine.

Out on the circuit, a GSX-R750R endurance model in competition and showing its close relationship to the stock machine.

Just as exciting was the RGV250 which replaced the older model in that class and featured a 90-degree, V-twin, two-stroke engine that embodied all the Suzuki knowledge of the engine type. The remainder of the machine was equally advanced, to offer a fast and responsive model able to perform to the highest standards.

The GSX750F was a new sports model, similar to the GSX600F, and combined the concept from that model with the technology from the GSX-R750. The latter was also imported into the UK in GSX-R750R form that was a pure race replica, technically street legal but only intended to be used on the track.

Less exotic, but intended for all-round use, was the GS500E that had a twin-cam, twin-cylinder engine fitted to a chassis using the usual Suzuki features. In a total contrast, the firm showed the NUDA, a concept model that embodied two-wheel drive, automatic transmission, power steering, a carbon fibre body and a swivelling seat as well as the usual high technology features. Aimed to take motorcycling into the next century, it certainly caused comment.

The GS500E was an all-round, mid-range model for most tasks; up-to-the-minute rather than exotic.

Radical new ideas were combined into the NUDA concept machine, some to come in the future, others to lead on into other directions.

INTO THE 1990s 1990-1996

The DR Big model was enlarged for 1990 to become the DR800S Desert Express, much as before but of 779cc capacity and with a number of minor improvements for its off-road use. The range of motocross and enduro machines continued with more new features to keep the firm in a leading position for any purpose from riding for fun to grand prix competition. Among the new models was the DR350M, first unveiled in the USA, which used a smaller version of the single-cylinder engine in a motocross chassis for serious off-road and enduro work.

For 1990 the Desert Express was enlarged to become the DR800S but kept its other features, including the protectors for rider and machine.

Smallest of the motocross range in the 1990s was this RM80 which used the same technology and style as the 125 and 250cc models.

The 1990 version of the TS125. Having been developed on further down the motocross route.

A competition enduro model, the DR350M, was first seen in the USA in 1990 and reached Europe the next year where it was equally well received.

A fresh scooter for 1990 was this AE50 model, listed as the 'Style', complete with the usual expected automatic features.

Retro style came to Suzuki with this 1990 VX800 roadster which combined the looks of the past with their V-twin engine.

The four-stroke, trail model range was extended in 1991 with the DR350S which followed the lines established by others in the series.

SUZUKI

RMX250M

The DR650 of 1991 fitted neatly between the other two trail singles and was just as fully equipped for its job.

For off-road enduro riders, the 1991 RMX250 took over from the old PE series and was based on the Suzuki which won the first world enduro title in 1990.

At the bottom end of the scale there was a new scooter, the AE50 that was given the name 'Style'. It was as automatic as it could be to suit its use in town, city or suburb. During the year it was joined by the VX800 roadster that adopted the popular retro style which was then appearing in contrast to the race replica and Paris-Dakar trends. Suzuki kept a touch of custom style for their offering by fitting their V-twin, eight-valve, water-cooled engine with its shaft drive in a chassis that reflected truely classic looks. Thus, it had twin rear shocks but lacked high bars, a seat backrest or forward pegs.

The trail range extended to add the DR350S in 1991, very much on the lines of the others in the series, while a mid-range model was added in the form of the DR650, the older DR600 Raider having been dropped in 1987. The old PE series was replaced by the RMX250M, a serious enduro model based on the machine which had won the first 250cc world enduro title the year before and a true competition animal.

The retro look took a real step forward with the GSX1100G that recalled the style of the GS1000 while employing the new technology of the 1990s. Rather different was the GSF400 Bandit for that had a twin-cam, four-cylinder, 16-valve engine red-lined at 14,000rpm, all hanging from a tubular trellis frame that employed the latest in suspension, wheels and brakes.

Recalling the style of the past, the GSX1100G of 1991 was in the retro mould but with ultra modern suspension and engine technology.

A new form for 1991 was the GSF400 Bandit with its four-cylinder engine hung from a tubular trellis frame.

Water-cooling finally came to the GSX-R750W in 1992 when that model took another step forward and adopted even more eye-catching graphics.

The custom V-twin became the VS800 for 1992 by adopting the VX800 engine to its shaft drive and street style.

One of the new 125cc models for 1992 was the RG125F Gamma which took that model further on with many changes.

Even more performance was offered in 1992 by the GSX-R750W, a further development of the series that introduced water-cooling while retaining the oil as a coolant. The whole engine was slimmer and more compact while the chassis was also further improved. For the custom rider there was the VS800 that used the engine from the retro VX800 while retaining the shaft drive and fixtures and fittings expected of the type.

The 1993 RF600R was a new form of super-sport model that combined a high-performance engine in an advanced chassis under a stylish fairing.

In 1994 the new concept was extended to introduce the RF900R that had the same technology and style but even more performance.

There were two new 125cc models, one the RG125F Gamma that came complete with a fairing, chassis, features and graphics that related to the firm's grand prix machines. The other, the RG125U Wolf, was equally new and shared the same engine and chassis but without a fairing or a crescent swing arm, being a concept aimed at a different market.

The super-sports range added the GSX-R1100W in the same format as the 750 of the previous year, but equally exciting was the RF600R. This brought an entirely fresh concept to Suzuki by combining a very high performance in a package well able to function from day to day with ease.

GN125

Commuters were offered the GN125 in retro style for 1994, the machine much on the lines of the 250 single.

The Bandit grew into the GSF600 for 1995 and gained a duplex cradle frame for its engine unit.

GSF600 BANDIT

Another custom V-twin model was added in 1995 as the VS600 that followed the style set by the 800 and 1400.

The AH100 was a new 1995 scooter that was powered by a two-stroke engine and had automatic transmission.

Inside a full fairing went a water-cooled, twin-cam, four-cylinder, 16-valve engine driving a six-speed gearbox. It incorporated all the latest advances from the firm and went into a chassis to suit. It proved to be a strong contender in the mid-range class.

For 1994 the concept was extended to add the RF900R on exactly the same lines and with the same result. To show that they listened to customers, the VS1400 was returned to the range, it having been dropped in 1991, still with three valves for each of its two cylinders and shaft drive. For commuters there was the economic GN125 with a single-cylinder, four-stroke engine.

An S2 version of the RF900R was added for 1995 and this had refinements for the suspension system and changes to both colours and graphics. A second Bandit appeared as the GSF600 which had a similar specification for the engine but a different frame of cradle form. The custom line of V-twins added the VS600 which continued the style of the larger models; meanwhile scooter riders were offered the AH100 and AN125 models. The first had a two-stroke engine, the second a four-stroke, but both featured electric start, automatic transmission and ample storage.

Top of the 1996 range was an all-new GSX-R750 that was even more compact, lighter and better faired for hyper performance on both the race track and the road. It epitomised the advanced technology of the leading machines.

Of equal interest, but in retro style, was the GSF600S Bandit that joined the existing model and came with a cockpit fairing. For retro riders seeking more capacity, Suzuki introduced the 1200 Bandit in plain form or with cockpit fairing to take over from the GSX1100G.

Off-road, the DR650SE was much revised and added an adjustable seat height to its features, while the RM125 and RM250 were further refined along with the RM80 to continue the motocross line. For the scooter rider there came the AP50, automatic and stylish.

The 1996 Suzuki range was extensive and covered their customers needs on road, race track, trail or motocross circuit, from hyper-sports to Paris-Dakar via mid-range, commuter, scooters, retro touring and custom. They sold worldwide with variants to suit local needs. Behind all stood a major firm that also built many other powered products. Truly, they had come a long way from the looms of Michio Suzuki.

Also new in 1995 was the AN125 scooter that had a single-cylinder, four-stroke engine but was otherwise much as the AH100 although the styling differed.

The fabulous GSX-R750 in its all-new 1996 form; slimmer, lighter and faster than ever before thanks to the highest technology.

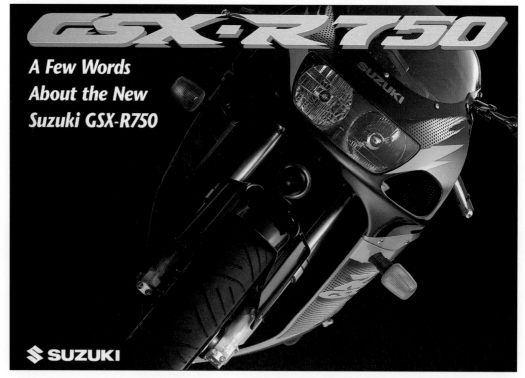

The GSF600S was a second version of the Bandit created for 1996 by adding a cockpit fairing.

Bandit N1200

Bandit S1200

A larger pair of Bandits for 1996 were the GSF1200, with or without the fairing, in the retro style.

For 1996 the DR650SE was revised and the seat provided a choice of two heights by means of a suspension adjustment.

The RM series for 1996, its concept and technology a far cry from that of two decades earlier and even further removed from the old TM models.

SUZUKI MODELS

No attempt will be made to list the hundreds of models built by Suzuki since 1952. Below are the basic types, most of which were built for several years, often with suffix codes to indicate minor changes or alternative specifications. The codes used prior to around 1970 have been omitted for clarity.

The lists that follow are arranged by engine cycle type, number of cylinders and intended purpose.

Two Strokes

Singles

Road
A50, AC50, AE50, AP50, AS50, CL50, CP50, CS50, F50, FR50, FS50, FZ50, GT50, K50, M50, U50, ZR50, A70, F70, FR70, U70, A80, CP80, CS80, FR80, K80, M80, A90, F90, K90, A100, AH100, B100, B100P, GP100, GP100U, GT100, B120, B120S, GP125, K125, RG125, RG125F, RG125U

Custom
OR50, ZR50L

Trail
MT50, RV50, TS50, RV75, TS75, RV90, TC90, TS90, TC100, TS100, KT120, TC120, K125, RV125, TC125, TS125, TC185, TS185, TS250, TS400

Motocross
RM50, TM75, RM80, RM100, TM100, RM125, TM125, RH250, RM250, TM250, RM400, RN400, TM400, RM500

Trial
RL250, RL325,

Enduro
PE175, PE250, RMX250M, PE400

Twins

Road
T90, GT125, T125, GT185, SB200, T200, X5, GT250, RG250, RGV250, T10, T20, T21, T250, X7, T305, T350, GT500, T500

Trail
TC200, TC250,

Triples

Road
GT380, GT550, GT750

Fours

Road
RG400, RG500

Four Strokes

Singles

Road	CO, COX, AN125, CS125, GN125, GS125, GS125ES
Custom	GN250, GN400, LS650,
Trail	DR125, DR350M, DR350S, SP370, DR400, SP400, DR600, DR650, DR650SE, DR750, DR800S

Twins

Road	GSX250, GSX250EZ, GS400, GSX400, GSX400EZ, GS425, GS450, GS450E, GS450TX, GS500E, VX800
Custom	GS250TT, GSX400T, GS450L, GS450T, VS600, VS750GL, VS800, VS1400, VS1400GL

Fours

Road	GSF400, GSX400F, GSX-R400, GSX-R400R, GS550, GS550M, GSX550E, GSF600, GSF600S, GSX600F, RF600R, GS650G, GS650GT, XN85, GS750, GSX750, GSX750E, GSX750F, GSX-R750, GSX-R750R, GSX-R750W, GS850G, RF900R, RF900RS2, GS1000, GS1000G, GS1000S, GSX1000S, GS1100G, GSX1100, GSX1100E, GSX1100EZ, GSX1100F, GSX1100G, GSX1100S, GSX-R1100, GSX-R1100W, GSF1200, GSF1200S, GV1400,
Custom	GS550L,

Rotary

Road	RE5